NURSERY
RHYMES

hinkler

Published by Hinkler Books Pty Ltd
45–55 Fairchild Street
Heatherton Victoria 3202 Australia
www.hinkler.com.au

hinkler

© Hinkler Books Pty Ltd 2006, 2011

Illustrators: Andrew Hopgood, Melissa Webb, Gerad Taylor,
Geoff Cook, Bill Wood, Anton Petrov and Marten Coombe
Prepress: Graphic Print Group
Typesetting: Graphicraft Limited

Images © Shutterstock.com: Seamless wallpaper pattern © Ozerina Anna;
Oval gold picture frame © Nodff.

ISBN: 978 1 7418 5019 2

Printed and bound in China

Contents

Contents

OLD KING COLE

Old King Cole
  Was a merry old soul,
And a merry old soul was he.
He called for his pipe,
And he called for his bowl,
And he called for his fiddlers three.
Every fiddler, he had a fiddle,
And a very fine fiddle had he;
Twee tweedle dee, tweedle dee,
  went the fiddlers.
Oh, there's none so rare,
As can compare
With King Cole and
  his fiddlers three.

THERE WAS AN OLD WOMAN
WHO LIVED IN A SHOE

There was an old woman
Who lived in a shoe,
She had so many children
She didn't know what to do;
She gave them some broth
Without any bread;
She scolded them soundly
And put them to bed.

HANDY SPANDY

Handy Spandy, Jack-a-dandy,
Loves plum cake and sugar candy.
He bought some at the grocer's shop,
And out he came, hop, hop, hop!

HUMPTY DUMPTY

Humpty Dumpty sat on a wall,
Humpty Dumpty had a great fall;
All the king's horses and all the king's men
Couldn't put Humpty together again.

CROSS-PATCH

Cross-patch, draw the latch,
Sit by the fire and spin;
Take a cup, and drink it up,
Then call your neighbours in.

ONE MISTY, MOISTY MORNING

One misty, moisty morning,
　　When cloudy was the weather,
I chanced to meet an old man
Clothed all in leather;
Clothed all in leather,
With cap under his chin.
'How do you do?' and 'How do you do?'
And 'How do you do?' again!

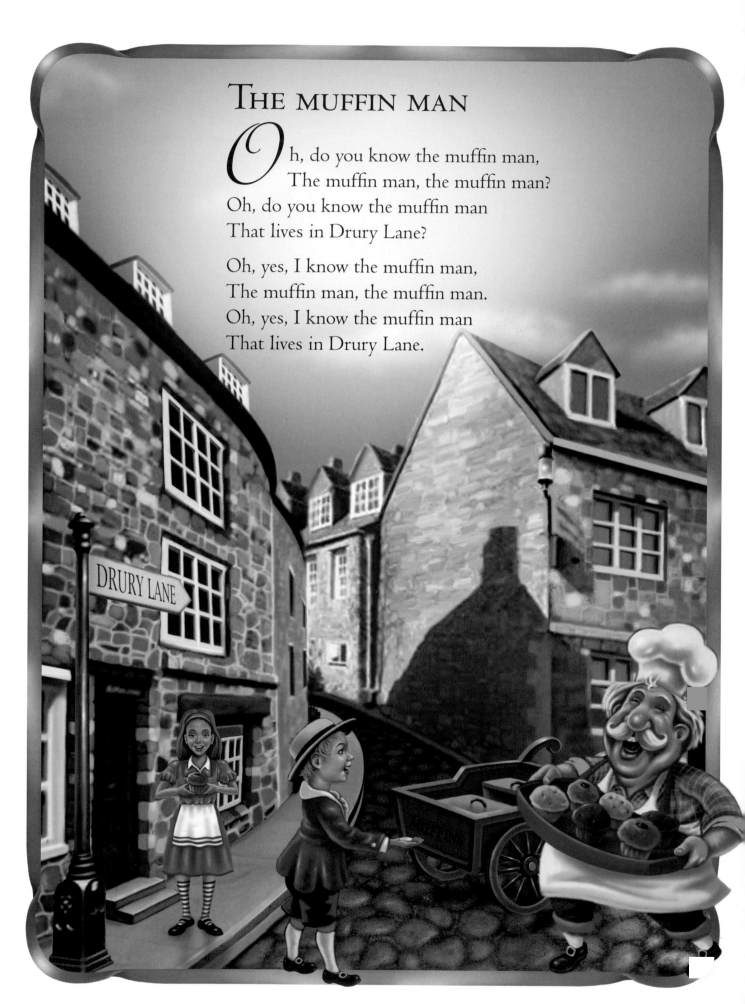

THE MUFFIN MAN

Oh, do you know the muffin man,
The muffin man, the muffin man?
Oh, do you know the muffin man
That lives in Drury Lane?

Oh, yes, I know the muffin man,
The muffin man, the muffin man.
Oh, yes, I know the muffin man
That lives in Drury Lane.

WEE WILLIE WINKIE

Wee Willie Winkie runs through the town,
Upstairs and downstairs in his nightgown,
Rapping at the window, crying through the lock,
'Are all the children in their beds,
It's past eight o'clock!'

The grand old Duke of York

Oh, the grand old Duke of York,
  He had ten thousand men;
He marched them up to the top of the hill,
And he marched them down again.
And when they were up, they were up,
And when they were down, they were down;
And when they were only halfway up,
They were neither up nor down.

OLD MCDONALD HAD A FARM

Old McDonald had a farm,
E-I-E-I-O!
And on that farm he had a cow,
E-I-E-I-O!
With a moo-moo here, and a moo-moo there,
Here a moo, there a moo,
Everywhere a moo-moo!
Old McDonald had a farm,
E-I-E-I-O!

Old McDonald had a farm,
E-I-E-I-O!
And on that farm he had a pig,
E-I-E-I-O!
With an oink-oink here, and an oink-oink there,
Here an oink, there an oink,
Everywhere an oink-oink!
Old McDonald had a farm,
E-I-E-I-O!

Old McDonald had a farm,
E-I-E-I-O!
And on that farm he had a horse,
E-I-E-I-O!
With a neigh-neigh here, and a neigh-neigh there,
Here a neigh, there a neigh,
Everywhere a neigh-neigh!
Old McDonald had a farm,
E-I-E-I-O!

Old McDonald had a farm,
E-I-E-I-O!
And on that farm he had some sheep,
E-I-E-I-O!
With a baa-baa here, and a baa-baa there,
Here a baa, there a baa,
Everywhere a baa-baa!
Old McDonald had a farm,
E-I-E-I-O!

Old McDonald had a farm,
E-I-E-I-O!
And on that farm he had a duck,
E-I-E-I-O!
With a quack-quack here,
and a quack-quack there,
Here a quack, there a quack,
Everywhere a quack-quack!
Old McDonald had a farm,
E-I-E-I-O!

Old McDonald had a farm,
E-I-E-I-O!
And on that farm he had a dog,
E-I-E-I-O!
With a woof-woof here, and a woof-woof there,
Here a woof, there a woof,
Everywhere a woof-woof!
Old McDonald had a farm,
E-I-E-I-O!

HICKETY, PICKETY

Hickety, pickety, my black hen,
  She lays eggs for gentlemen;
Gentlemen come every day
To see what my black hen doth lay;
Sometimes nine and sometimes ten,
Hickety, pickety, my black hen.

For want of a nail

For want of a nail, the shoe was lost;

For want of the shoe, the horse was lost;

For want of the horse, the rider was lost;

For want of the rider, the battle was lost;

For want of the battle, the kingdom was lost;

And all from the want of a horseshoe nail.

GOOSEY, GOOSEY GANDER

Goosey, goosey gander,
　　Whither shall I wander?
Upstairs and downstairs
And in my lady's chamber;
There I met an old man
Who would not say his prayers;
I took him by the left leg
And threw him down the stairs.

HIGGLETY, PIGGLETY, POP!

Higglety, pigglety, pop!
The dog has eaten the mop;
The pig's in a hurry,
The cat's in a flurry,
Higglety, pigglety, pop!

LITTLE BO-PEEP

Little Bo-Peep has lost her sheep,
And can't tell where to find them;
Leave them alone, and they'll come home,
And bring their tails behind them.

Little Bo-Peep fell fast asleep,
And dreamed she heard them bleating;
But when she awoke she found it a joke,
For they were still a-fleeting.

Then up she took her little crook,
Determined for to find them;
She found them indeed, but it made her heart bleed,
For they'd left their tails behind them.

It happened one day, as Bo-Peep did stray
Into a meadow hard by,
There she spied their tails side by side,
All hung on a tree to dry.

She heaved a sigh, and wiped her eye,
And over the hillocks went rambling,
And tried what she could, as a shepherdess should,
To tack each again to its lambkin.

I HAD A LITTLE HEN

I had a little hen,
The prettiest ever seen;
She washed up the dishes,
And kept the house clean.
She went to the mill
To fetch me some flour,
She brought it home
In less than an hour.
She baked me my bread,
She brewed me my ale,
She sat by the fire
And told many a fine tale.

TO MARKET, TO MARKET

To market, to market, to buy a fat pig,
Home again, home again, jiggety-jig;
To market, to market, to buy a fat hog,
Home again, home again, jiggety-jog.
To market, to market, to buy a plum bun;
Home again, home again, market is done.

MARY HAD A LITTLE LAMB

Mary had a little lamb,
Its fleece was white as snow;
And everywhere that Mary went
The lamb was sure to go.

It followed her to school one day,
Which was against the rule;
It made the children laugh and play
To see a lamb at school.

And so the teacher turned it out,
But still it lingered near,
And waited patiently about
Till Mary did appear.

'What makes the lamb love Mary so?'
The eager children cry;
'Why, Mary loves the lamb, you know,'
The teacher did reply.

THREE BLIND MICE

Three blind mice, see how they run!
They all ran after the farmer's wife,
Who cut off their tails with a carving knife;
Did you ever see such a thing in your life,
As three blind mice?

I ASKED MY MOTHER
FOR FIFTY CENTS

I asked my mother for fifty cents,
  To see the elephant jump the fence,
He jumped so high,
He reached the sky,
And didn't come back till the fourth of July.

POLLY PUT THE KETTLE ON

Polly, put the kettle on,
    Polly, put the kettle on,
Polly, put the kettle on,
We'll all have tea.

Sukey, take it off again,
Sukey, take it off again,
Sukey, take it off again,
They've all gone away.

If all the world was apple pie

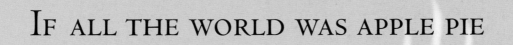

If all the world was apple pie,

And all the sea was ink,

And all the trees were bread and cheese,

What should we have to drink?

SING A SONG OF SIXPENCE

Sing a song of sixpence,
　A pocket full of rye;
Four and twenty blackbirds
Baked in a pie.

When the pie was opened
The birds began to sing;
Wasn't that a dainty dish
To set before the king?

The king was in his counting-house
Counting out his money;
The queen was in the parlour
Eating bread and honey.

The maid was in the garden
Hanging out the clothes,
When down came a blackbird,
And pecked off her nose.

JELLY ON A PLATE

Jelly on a plate,
Jelly on a plate,
Wibble, wobble, wibble, wobble,
Jelly on a plate.

LITTLE JACK HORNER

Little Jack Horner
Sat in a corner,
Eating a Christmas pie;
He put in his thumb,
And pulled out a plum,
And said, 'What a
good boy am I!'

A WAS AN APPLE PIE

 *A* was an apple pie

 B bit it

C cut it

D dealt it

E eat it

F fought for it

G got it

 H had it

I inspected it

J jumped for it

K kept it

L longed for it

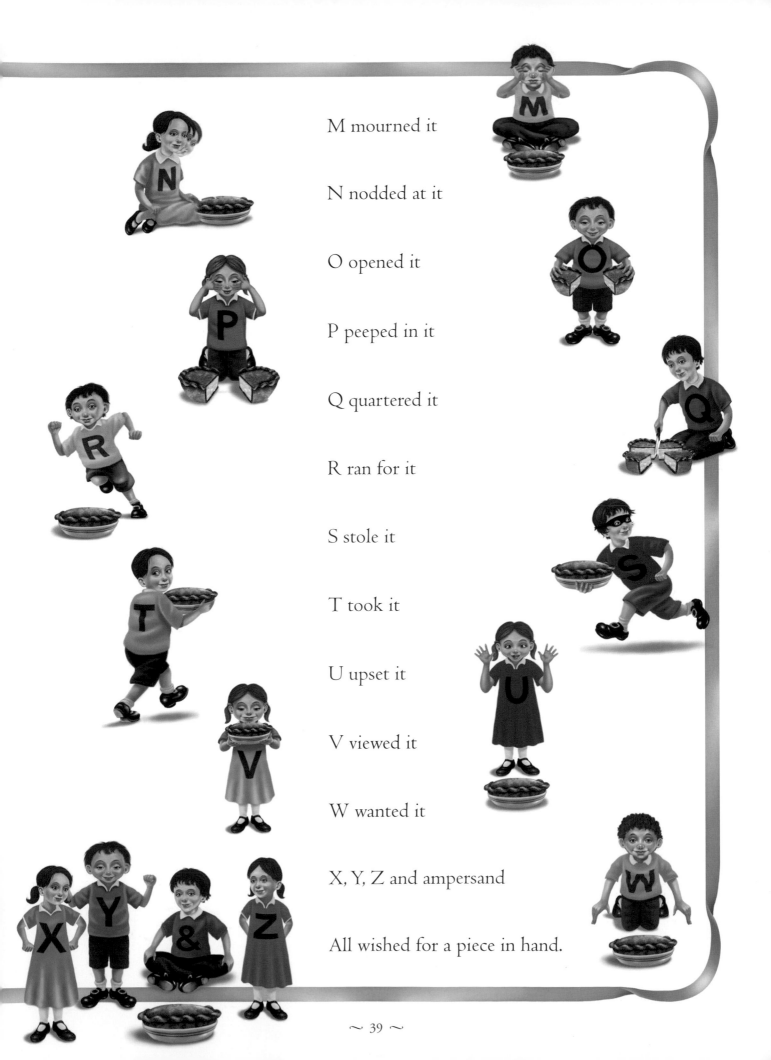

M mourned it

N nodded at it

O opened it

P peeped in it

Q quartered it

R ran for it

S stole it

T took it

U upset it

V viewed it

W wanted it

X, Y, Z and ampersand

All wished for a piece in hand.

ROCK-A-BYE, BABY, ON THE TREE TOP

Rock-a-bye, baby, on the tree top,
When the wind blows, the cradle will rock;
When the bough breaks, the cradle will fall,
Down will come baby, cradle and all.

DANCE, LITTLE BABY

Dance, little baby, dance up high!
Never mind, baby, Mother is by.
Crow and caper, caper and crow,
There, little baby, there you go.
Up to the ceiling, down to the ground,
Backwards and forwards, round and round!
Dance, little baby, and Mother shall sing,
With the merry chorus, ding-a-ding, ding.

Hush, little baby

Hush, little baby, don't say a word,
Papa's going to buy you a mocking bird.

If that mocking bird won't sing,
Papa's going to buy you a diamond ring.

If that diamond ring turns brass,
Papa's going to buy you a looking glass.

If that looking glass gets broke,
Papa's going to buy you a billy goat.

If that billy goat won't pull,
Papa's going to buy you a cart and bull.

If that cart and bull turn over,
Papa's going to buy you a dog named Rover.

If that dog named Rover won't bark,
Papa's going to buy you a horse and cart.

If that horse and cart fall down,
You'll still be the sweetest little baby in town.

I had a little nut tree

I had a little nut tree,
　　Nothing would it bear
But a silver nutmeg
And a golden pear.

The King of Spain's daughter
Came to visit me,
And all for the sake
Of my little nut tree.

I skipped over water,
I danced over sea;
And all the birds in the air
Couldn't catch me!

MARY, MARY, QUITE CONTRARY

Mary, Mary, quite contrary,
How does your garden grow?
With silver bells and cockle shells,
And pretty maids all in a row.

HERE WE GO ROUND THE MULBERRY BUSH

Here we go round the mulberry bush,
The mulberry bush, the mulberry bush.
Here we go round the mulberry bush,
On a cold and frosty morning.

This is the way we wash our clothes,
Wash our clothes, wash our clothes.
This is the way we wash our clothes,
On a cold and frosty morning.

I HEAR THUNDER

I hear thunder,
I hear thunder;
Hark, don't you,
Hark, don't you?
Pitter-patter raindrops,
Pitter-patter raindrops;
I'm wet through,
So are you!

I see blue skies,
I see blue skies,
Way up high,
Way up high;
Hurry up the sunshine,
Hurry up the sunshine;
We'll soon dry,
We'll soon dry!

GIRLS AND BOYS, COME OUT TO PLAY

Girls and boys, come out to play,
The moon doth shine as bright as day.
Leave your supper and leave your sleep,
And join your playfellows into the street.
Come with a whoop and come with a call,
Come with a good will or not at all.
Up the ladder and down the wall,
A half-penny loaf will serve us all;
You find milk and I'll find flour,
And we'll have a pudding in half an hour.

LITTLE BOY BLUE

Little Boy Blue,
      Come blow your horn,
The sheep's in the meadow,
The cow's in the corn.

Where is the boy
Who looks after the sheep?
He's under the haystack,
Fast asleep.

Will you wake him?
No, not I,
For if I do,
He's sure to cry.

There was a little girl

There was a little girl, and she had a little curl
    Right in the middle of her forehead;
When she was good, she was very, very good,
But when she was bad, she was horrid.

SALLY, GO ROUND THE SUN

Sally, go round the sun,
  Sally, go round the moon,
Sally, go round the chimneypots,
On a Saturday afternoon.

GEORGIE PORGIE

Georgie Porgie, pudding and pie,
   Kissed the girls and made them cry;
When the boys came out to play,
Georgie Porgie ran away.

LITTLE TOMMY TUCKER

Little Tommy Tucker
Sings for his supper;
What shall he eat?
Brown bread and butter.
How shall he cut it
Without e'er a knife?
How will he be married
Without e'er a wife?

DIDDLE, DIDDLE, DUMPLING, MY SON JOHN

Diddle, diddle, dumpling, my son John,
Went to bed with his trousers on;
One shoe off, and one shoe on,
Diddle, diddle, dumpling, my son John.

JACK, BE NIMBLE

Jack, be nimble,
Jack, be quick,
Jack, jump over
The candlestick.

Tom, Tom, the Piper's Son

Tom, Tom, the piper's son
Stole a pig and away did run;
The pig was eat
And Tom was beat,
And Tom went howling down the street.

WHAT ARE LITTLE BOYS MADE OF?

What are little boys made of, made of?
What are little boys made of?
Frogs and snails and puppy dogs' tails,
That's what little boys are made of.

What are little girls made of, made of?
What are little girls made of?
Sugar and spice and all things nice,
That's what little girls are made of.

HERE ARE GRANDMA'S GLASSES

Here are Grandma's glasses,
Here is Grandma's hat,
This is the way she folds her hands,
And puts them in her lap.

Here are Grandpa's glasses,
Here is Grandpa's hat,
This is the way he folds his arms,
And takes a little nap.

INCY WINCY SPIDER

Incy Wincy Spider
    Climbed up the water spout.
Down came the rain
And washed poor Incy out.

Out came the sunshine
And dried up all the rain,
And Incy Wincy Spider
Climbed up the spout again.

THIS LITTLE PIGGY

This little piggy went to market,
This little piggy stayed at home;
This little piggy had roast beef,
This little piggy had none;
And this little piggy cried,
'Wee-wee-wee,'
All the way home.

OLD MOTHER HUBBARD

Old Mother Hubbard
   Went to the cupboard
To fetch her poor dog a bone;
But when she got there,
The cupboard was bare,
And so the poor dog had none.

She went to the baker's
To buy him some bread;
But when she came back
The poor dog was dead.

She went to the undertaker's
To buy him a coffin;
But when she came back
The poor dog was laughing.

She went to the fishmonger's
To buy him some fish;
But when she came back
He was washing the dish.

She went to the tavern
For white wine and red;
But when she came back
The dog stood on his head.

She went to the hatter's
To buy him a hat;
But when she came back
He was feeding the cat.

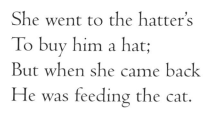

She went to the barber's
To buy him a wig;
But when she came back,
He was dancing a jig.

She went to the fruiterer's
To buy him some fruit;
But when she came back,
He was playing the flute.

She went to the tailor's
To buy him a coat;
But when she came back
He was riding a goat.

She went to the cobbler's
To buy him some shoes,
But when she came back
He was reading the news.

She went to the seamstress
To buy him some linen;
But when she came back
The dog was a-spinning.

She went to the hosier's
To buy him some hose;
But when she came back
He was dressed in his clothes.

The dame made a curtsy,
The dog made a bow;
The dame said, 'Your servant!'
The dog said, 'Bow-wow.'

HICKORY, DICKORY, DOCK

Hickory, dickory, dock,
The mouse ran up the clock,
The clock struck one,
The mouse ran down,
Hickory, dickory, dock.

THE DOVE SAYS, 'COO, COO'

The dove says, 'Coo, coo, what shall I do?
I can scarce maintain two.'
'Pooh! Pooh!' says the wren; 'I have got ten,
And keep them all like gentlemen.'

LITTLE SALLY WATERS

Little Sally Waters,
Sitting in the sun,
Crying and weeping,
For a young man.
Rise, Sally, rise,
Dry your weeping eyes,
Fly to the east,
Fly to the west,
Fly to the one you love the best.

CURLY LOCKS

Curly Locks! Curly Locks! Will you be mine?
You shall not wash dishes, nor yet feed the swine,
But sit on a cushion and sew a fine seam,
And feed upon strawberries, sugar and cream.

Where are you going, my pretty maid?

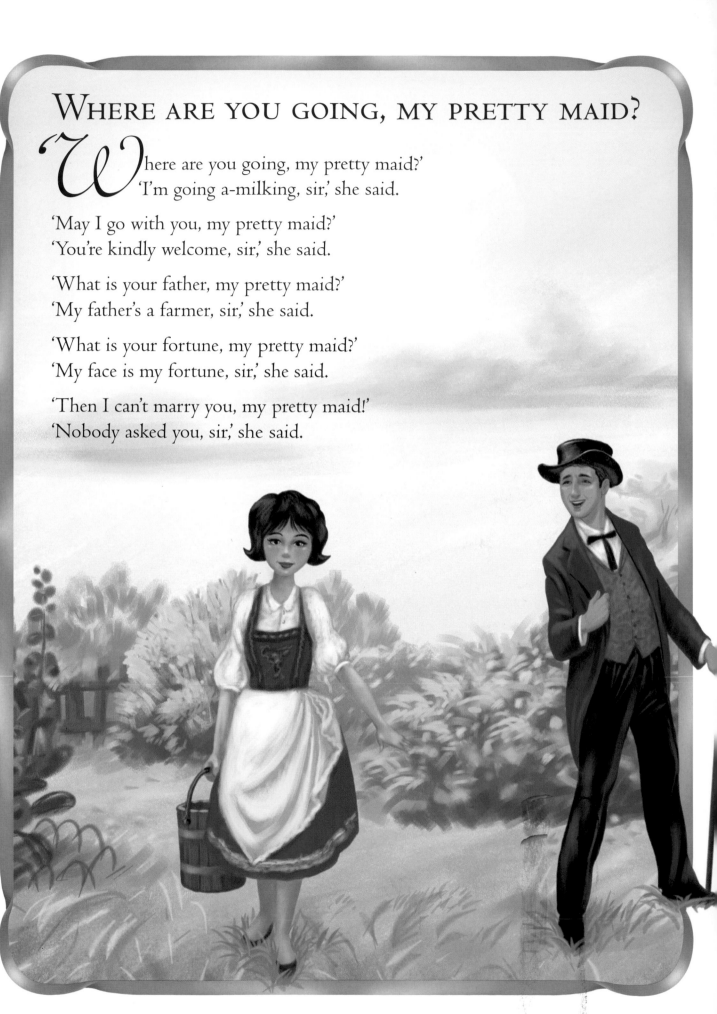

'Where are you going, my pretty maid?'
'I'm going a-milking, sir,' she said.

'May I go with you, my pretty maid?'
'You're kindly welcome, sir,' she said.

'What is your father, my pretty maid?'
'My father's a farmer, sir,' she said.

'What is your fortune, my pretty maid?'
'My face is my fortune, sir,' she said.

'Then I can't marry you, my pretty maid!'
'Nobody asked you, sir,' she said.

Tommy Snooks and Bessy Brooks

As Tommy Snooks and Bessy Brooks
Were walking out one Sunday,
Says Tommy Snooks to Bessy Brooks,
'Tomorrow will be Monday.'

ONE, TWO, THREE, FOUR, FIVE

One, two, three, four, five,
    Once I caught a fish alive;
Six, seven, eight, nine, ten,
Then I let it go again.

Why did you let it go?
Because it bit my finger so.
Which finger did it bite?
This little finger on the right.

HERE IS THE BEEHIVE

Here is the beehive,
But where are all the bees?
Hiding away where nobody sees.

Here they come creeping
Out of their hive,
One and two and three, four, five.

There were ten in the bed

There were ten in the bed
And the little one said,
'Roll over! Roll over!'
So they all rolled over
And one fell out,
And he gave a little scream,
And he gave a little shout, 'Yahoo!'
Please remember to tie a knot in
    your pyjamas,
Single beds are only made for
One, two, three, four, five, six, seven, eight –

There were nine in the bed
And the little one said,
'Roll over! Roll over!'
So they all rolled over
And one fell out,
And he gave a little scream,
And he gave a little shout, 'Yahoo!'
Please remember to tie a knot in your pyjamas,
Single beds are only made for
One, two, three, four, five, six, seven –

There were eight in the bed
And the little one said,
'Roll over! Roll over!'
So they all rolled over
And one fell out,
And he gave a little scream,
And he gave a little shout, 'Yahoo!'
Please remember to tie a knot in your pyjamas,
Single beds are only made for
One, two, three, four, five, six –

There were seven in the bed
And the little one said,
'Roll over! Roll over!'
So they all rolled over
And one fell out,
And he gave a little scream,
And he gave a little shout, 'Yahoo!'
Please remember to tie a knot in
    your pyjamas,
Single beds are only made for
One, two, three, four, five –

There were six in the bed
And the little one said,
'Roll over! Roll over!'
So they all rolled over
And one fell out,
And he gave a little scream,
And he gave a little shout, 'Yahoo!'
Please remember to tie a knot in
    your pyjamas,
Single beds are only made for
One, two, three, four —

There were five in the bed
And the little one said,
'Roll over! Roll over!'
So they all rolled over
And one fell out,
And he gave a little scream,
And he gave a little shout, 'Yahoo!'
Please remember to tie a knot in
   your pyjamas,
Single beds are only made for
One, two, three —

There were four in the bed
And the little one said,
'Roll over! Roll over!'
So they all rolled over
And one fell out,
And he gave a little scream,
And he gave a little shout, 'Yahoo!'
Please remember to tie a knot in
   your pyjamas,
Single beds are only made for
One, two —

There were three in the bed
And the little one said,
'Roll over! Roll over!'
So they all rolled over
And one fell out,
And he gave a little scream,
And he gave a little shout, 'Yahoo!'
Please remember to tie a knot in
   your pyjamas,
Single beds are only made for
One —

There were two in the bed
And the little one said,
'Roll over! Roll over!'
So they all rolled over
And one fell out,
And he gave a little scream,
And he gave a little shout, 'Yahoo!'
Please remember to tie a knot in
    your pyjamas,
Single beds are only made for one.
Single beds are only made for one.

Thirty Days Hath September

Thirty days hath September,
April, June and November;
February has twenty-eight alone,
All the rest have thirty-one,
Excepting leap-year – that's the time,
When February's days are twenty-nine.

FIVE FAT SAUSAGES

Five fat sausages frying in a pan,
One went pop!
And then it went bang!

Four fat sausages frying in a pan,
One went pop!
And then it went bang!

Three fat sausages frying in a pan,
One went pop!
And then it went bang!

Two fat sausages frying in a pan,
One went pop!
And then it went bang!

One fat sausage frying in a pan,
One went pop!
And then it went bang!

And there were no sausages left!

THE FLYING PIG

Dickery, dickery, dare,
The pig flew up in the air;
The man in brown
Soon brought him down.
Dickery, dickery, dare.

PUSSYCAT, PUSSYCAT

Pussycat, pussycat, where have you been?
    I've been to London to visit the queen.
Pussycat, pussycat, what did you there?
I frightened a little mouse under her chair.

As I was going to St Ives

As I was going to St Ives,
I met a man with seven wives.
Each wife had seven sacks.
Each sack had seven cats.
Each cat had seven kits.
Kits, cats, sacks and wives:
How many were going to St Ives?

THE BIG SHIP SAILS ON THE ALLEY, ALLEY O

The big ship sails on the alley, alley O,
The alley, alley O, the alley, alley O.
The big ship sails on the alley, alley O,
On the last day of September.

The captain said, 'It will never, never do,
Never never do, never never do.'
The captain said, 'It will never, never do,'
On the last day of September.

The big ship sank to the bottom of the sea,
The bottom of the sea, the bottom of the sea,
The big ship sank to the bottom of the sea,
On the last day of September.

We all dip our heads in the deep, blue sea.
The deep, blue sea, the deep, blue sea.
We all dip our heads in the deep, blue sea,
On the last day of September.

Row, row, row your boat

Row, row, row your boat,
Gently down the stream,
Merrily, merrily, merrily, merrily,
Life is but a dream.

Doctor Foster

Doctor Foster went to Gloucester
  In a shower of rain;
He stepped in a puddle,
Right up to his middle,
And never went there again.

How many miles to Babylon?

How many miles to Babylon?
   Three score miles and ten.
Can I get there by candlelight?
Yes, and back again.
If your heels be nimble and light,
You may get there by candlelight.

BABYLON

STAR WISH

Star light, star bright,
First star I see tonight,
I wish I may, I wish I might,
Have the wish I wish tonight.

GOODNIGHT, SLEEP TIGHT

Goodnight, sleep tight,
    Wake up bright
In the morning light,
To do what's right
With all your might.

AND SO GOODNIGHT!

Here's a body – there's a bed!
There's a pillow – here's a head!
There's a curtain – here's a light!
There's a puff – and so goodnight!

The man in the moon

The man in the moon looked out of the moon,
And this is what he said:
'Now that I'm getting up, 'tis time
All children went to bed!'